AF538342

Printed in Toronto, Canada. The Strategic Coach Inc., 33 Fraser Avenue, Suite 201, Toronto, Ontario, M6K 3J9.

If you would like further information about The Strategic Coach® Program or other Strategic Coach® services and products, please telephone 416.531.7399 or 1.800.387.3206.

Library and Archives Canada Cataloguing in Publication

Sullivan, Dan, 1944-, author
The 80% approach / Dan Sullivan.

ISBN 978-1-897239-29-2 (bound)

1. Success--Psychological aspects. 2. Work--Psychological aspects. 3. Problem solving. I. Title. II. Title: Eighty percent approach.

BF481.S85 2013 158.7 C2013-903226-6

Contents

Being Entrepreneurial

Taking all of the resources in your personal and work life to higher levels of productivity.

I coach entrepreneurs, and our company, Strategic Coach®, makes it faster and easier for thousands of highly successful entrepreneurs and their teams to multiply their performance, results, success, and satisfaction with truly unique and effective concepts and tools. The 80% Approach™ is one of those concepts and tools, and as you will discover, it can be very powerful and motivating.

This book, however, is not just for actual entrepreneurs and entrepreneurial companies, but for any individual, group, team, or organization in the world that is entrepreneurial in thought, communication, and aspiration.

By "entrepreneurial," I go back to the original 1804 definition by French economist Jean-Baptiste Say who described an entrepreneur as *someone who takes resources from a lower level to a higher level of productivity.* In other words, entrepreneurially-minded individuals are those who continually strive to make things more useful and valuable than they found them. And they are groups, teams, and organizations that strive to create new structures and processes in the world that make things better for everyone.

The 80% Approach that I describe in this book is a transformative way of thinking, communicating, and achieving for everyone on the planet who is entrepreneurially-minded in the 21st century.

Writing to you personally, right here, I predict you will find that the next half-hour or so it takes you to read this little book may be one of the best investments of your time and attention in your entire lifetime.

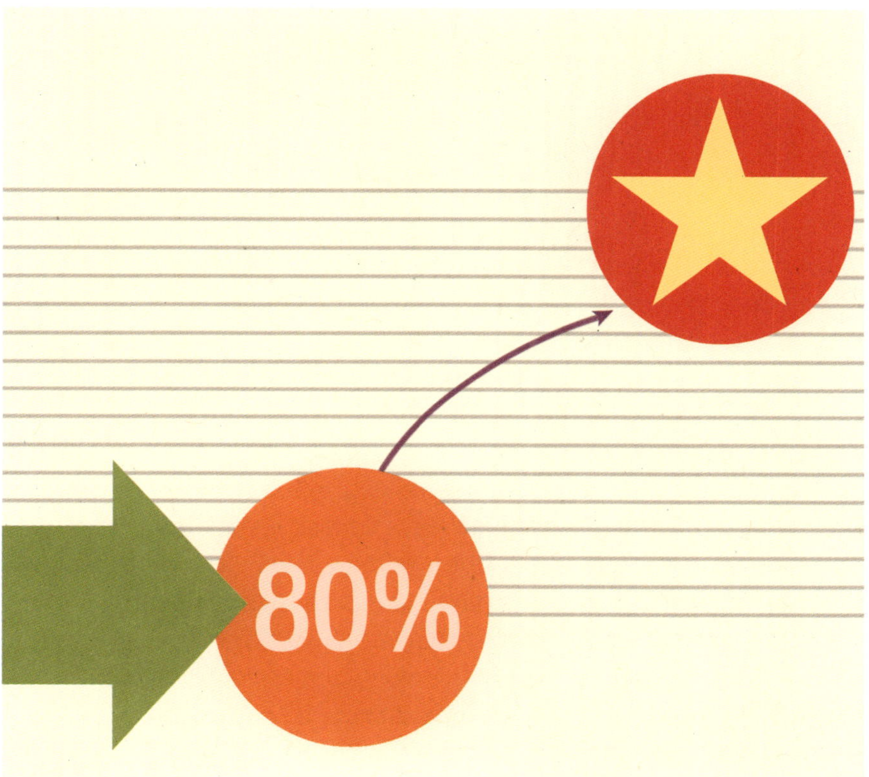

Certainly, I predict it will be one of the greatest investments for your much bigger and better future. Since I started coaching entrepreneurs in 1974, I have become convinced that the most innovative and successful entrepreneurs in the world, the men and women who consistently create great value in the marketplace over their entire lives, are also the best "80%" people in the world.

Entrepreneurial foundation.

To understand what that means for them, and what it can now mean for you, I invite you to make The 80% Approach a fundamental foundation for all of your personal and work activities and situations, so that "being entrepreneurial" increasingly characterizes all of your successes in the years ahead.

The 80% Approach™

A way of thinking and acting that eliminates the paralysis of perfectionism and procrastination.

I start my explanation of The 80% Approach with a warning: The solution it offers is so simple and obvious that you may discount and ignore it. Here's how this remarkably simple concept and method will help you eliminate perfectionism and procrastination for the rest of your life.

The 80% breakthrough for a lifetime of confident achievement.
On the facing page is a diagram of a square that has been divided into six "80%" sections. Each of these sections represents a stage of human effort and activity, and the whole square represents a single project. From this simple diagram, we can develop an entire philosophy and methodology for achieving results—without any procrastination. If you master and apply the meaning and implications of this single diagram, you will effectively eliminate all perfectionism and procrastination in your life on a continual basis.

The first 80% is often good enough.
The largest box in the diagram represents our first attempt at doing a project—any kind of project in our lives. It says that the first time we do anything, when we finish judging our effort, it is 80% of the way there, no matter how much preparation we do before taking action. We see it as only 80% because as we were completing the project, we immediately saw all kinds of ways that it could have been better. The first-attempt result may be great, but in our minds it's only 80% of the way there.

Is one 80% attempt good enough? In many situations in life, just doing 80% the first time is good enough. You don't have to go any further. People who are perfectionists, of course, would never accept this. They keep working on the project, making endless improvements until

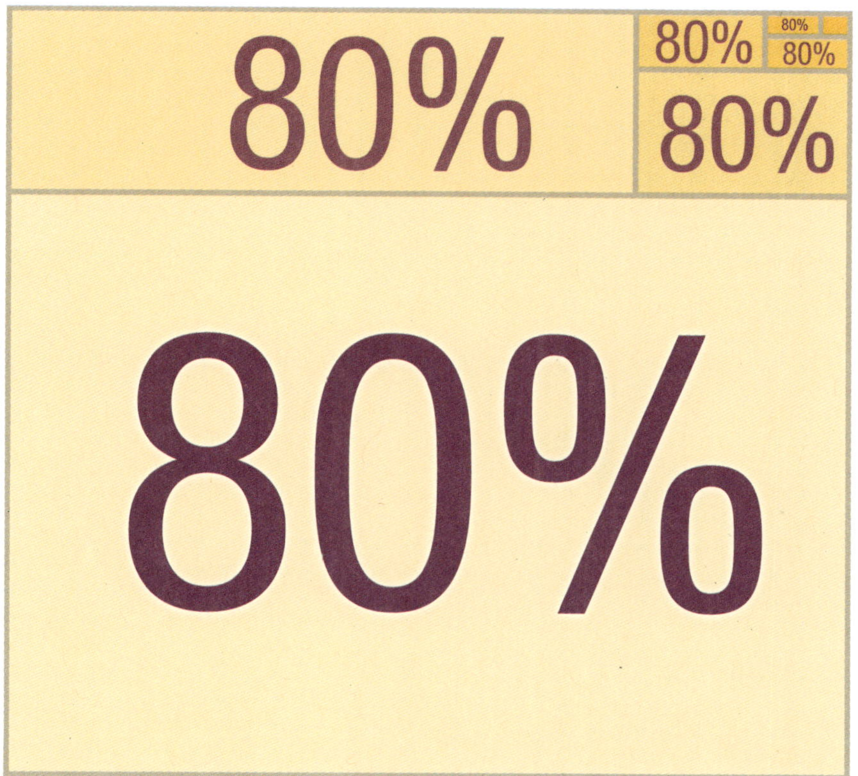

it is "perfect"—even though none of this extra work is necessary. This has nothing to do with the project itself or its usefulness to other people. It only has to do with what is going on inside of the perfectionist's mind. The 80% Approach, then, gives us permission to nip perfectionism in the bud. If 80% is good enough, then that's the very best result we need to achieve.

Get the first 80% result as quickly as possible.
Since just one 80% result may be all that's needed, it makes all the sense in the world to get it done as quickly as possible so we can benefit from the result. If more than one 80% attempt is needed, it's also important to achieve the first 80% result quickly so we can start

involving the capabilities of other people in the overall project.

The second 80%.
This can represent further improvements to the project on our part or, even better, further improvements done by other talented people. Even though this is called "the second 80%," it actually brings the overall project to 96% of the ideal result.

Are two 80% attempts all that's needed? In all but a few situations in life, the answer is "yes." In a world filled with many sub-standard, shoddy, and unsatisfactory results, a 96%-quality project would look and actually be extraordinary.

Delegate the second 80% attempt as much as possible: When more than one 80% attempt is necessary to produce a satisfactory result in the world, it's crucial to delegate as much as possible to other people who have even better talents and capabilities than we do. This infusion of new abilities rapidly increases the quality of the overall result.

Three or more 80% achievements.
Although just two 80% attempts would be satisfactory in most projects, there are some areas—for example, surgical procedures and manufacturing processes—where as many as six 80% attempts are necessary to guarantee a minimally acceptable level of quality. These further attempts are indicated on the diagram by the four increasingly smaller 80% boxes in the upper-right corner of the square.

Understanding perfectionism and procrastination—then moving on.
In this book, I will identify eight extraordinary advantages of The 80% Approach. Before getting to them, let's just spend a few pages understanding why people get trapped in perfectionism and procrastination.

Perfectionism And Procrastination

Two paralyzing traps that always undermine individual and organizational confidence.

The human brain is capable of extraordinary creativity and inventiveness. Our lives today provide us with overwhelming proof of a history of great breakthroughs and progress in all fields of endeavor. All of these achievements were generated by unique ideas of countless intelligent men and women. At the same time, the power of the human brain can work against itself in ways that leave many people feeling chronically guilty and dissatisfied—in spite of living in a world of great achievements. With seemingly everything in the world to be optimistic about, many people are frustrated and non-productive throughout much of their lives. What accounts for this paralysis of thinking and action when so many opportunities for personal confidence and productivity are available?

Two mental habits that can paralyze us for an entire lifetime. The answer lies in the realm of habits—mental habits that are just the opposite of creativity and inventiveness. Two in particular, perfectionism and procrastination, are perhaps the biggest factors in the undermining of personal confidence and motivation. The habit of perfectionism paralyzes our ability to make decisions and commitments, while the habit of procrastination paralyzes our ability to take action. *Perfectionism is the result of a mental obsession with achieving the "ideal"—as a minimum requirement—in all situations and areas of life. Procrastination results from the refusal to take action until an "ideal" result is guaranteed in every situation.* These two habits almost always accompany each other. You seldom have one without the other.

Two negative habits that continually reinforce each other.
Perfectionists are always procrastinators, and procrastinators are always perfectionists. All individuals have some perfectionism and procrastination in their make-up—even if in very small amounts—but for some people these two habits dominate their thinking and action over their entire lifetime. As a result, they always have chronically low personal confidence, and this will never improve until these paralyzing habits are eliminated.

Perfectionism: obsession with the "ideal."
Perfectionism represents a belief system about how life should work—not how it actually does work. This is a crucial point. Perfectionists live in an all-encompassing world of "shoulds." They especially direct this toward themselves. They "should" be this, they "should" have done that, this "shouldn't" have happened to them. And, in every case, what actually did happen never measures up to their judgment about what should have happened. Perfectionism leads to a perpetual dissatisfaction with the past and pessimism about the future. In both cases, past and future, as well as the present, perfectionists never take ownership of what happens to them.

Procrastination: refusal to take action.
Procrastinators insist on guarantees before taking action in a world that doesn't provide any guarantees. They continually end up feeling guilty over their stupidity, and yet they keep emotionally insisting on the guarantees. Because of their obsession with perfectionism, they find it difficult to make a decision or a commitment unless they can be certain it will lead to an "ideal" result. Out of necessity, they have to produce some results in life just to make an income, but it's always a struggle. Procrastinators are their own worst enemies because they undermine their own confidence and cut themselves off from opportunities, resources, and capabilities that other people could provide to them—if only they would take action at the appropriate time.

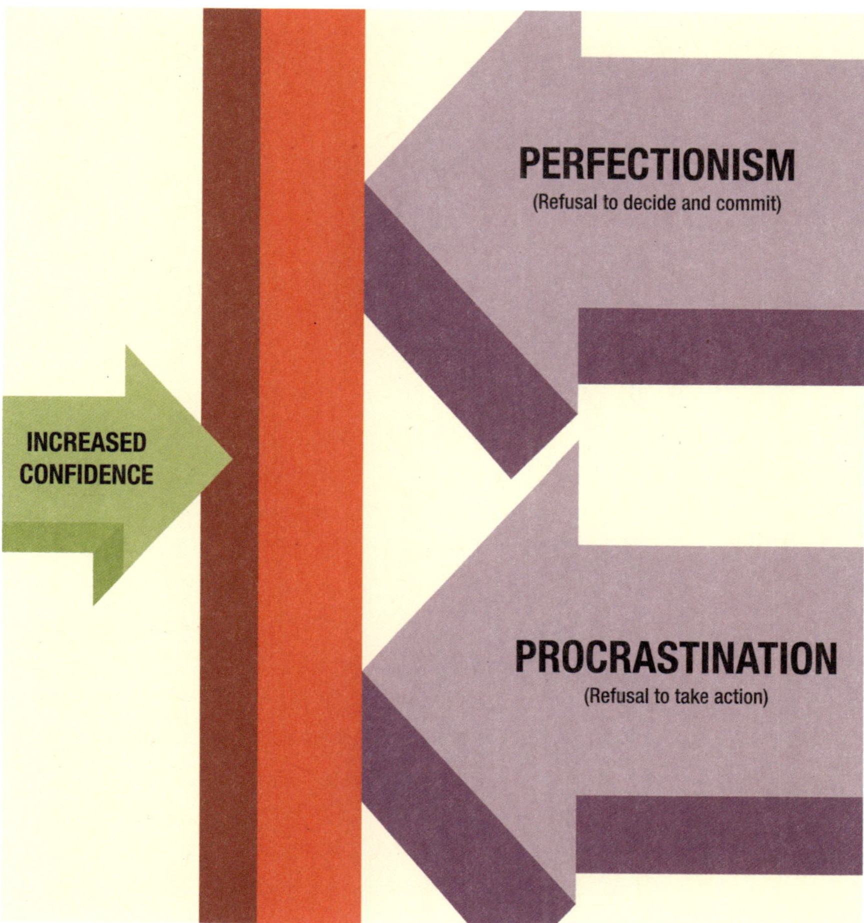

Everyone who wants to can break out of these traps.
These two obstacles to individual confidence—perfectionism and procrastination—are universal maladies. With rare exceptions, every human being suffers from them at some point in life. A solution to both obstacles would be extraordinarily valuable, not only for the individuals themselves, but for the world as a whole. On the following pages, we'll examine a concept and method, "The 80% Approach," that seeks to provide such a solution. Anyone who is willing can utilize this solution in a remarkably short time.

Advantage 1

The first attempt at anything is never more than 80% — regardless of preparation.

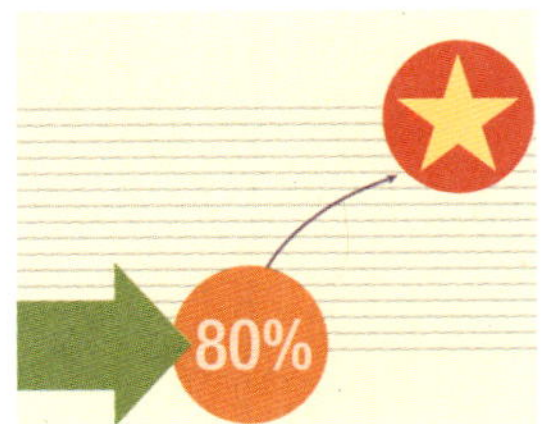

I've noticed something about my experiences with trying to get projects done. If I just jump into the project and finish it as quickly as possible, my self-judgment when I'm finished is that the result was only "80% good enough."

If, on the other hand, I procrastinate for a long time, feeling that I am not prepared to launch into the project, when I actually do complete it, my self-judgment is also that the result was only 80%. And, if I take weeks to think through the project, attempting to be as prepared as possible, my self-judgment when I complete it is that the result is still only 80%. No matter how I approach the project, my self-judgment about the result is always the same.

Confidence only comes from fast engagement and completion. Why is my self-judgment always 80%? I think the answer lies in what happens to my thinking, and yours, when we're actually engaged in completing a project. We start with an idea of the best way to complete the project and what the best result should be. As soon as we're engaged, however, our understanding of what is involved and needed expands, deepens, and transforms. But none of this new learning can take place until engagement starts.

Regardless of whether we're procrastinating or trying to be more prepared, little or no learning takes place until we actually start.

Something powerful happens to the mind and emotions when we're engaged in producing a practical result. We become focused, blocking out other possibilities. We begin utilizing all of our intelligence and creativity. And we feel a sense of urgency, risk, and excitement.

Why procrastination is always doubly bad for us.
Procrastination—which I contend is based on judging ourselves by a standard of perfection—is always counterproductive in two particularly harmful ways. First, it robs us of personal confidence during the period before we become engaged with the project. When we procrastinate about a particular project, it's because we don't feel confident enough to take it on. But by procrastinating, we take away any confidence we do have. It makes getting started doubly difficult from an emotional and psychological standpoint. Second, when we actually do engage with the project, we feel a sense of personal loss and guilt about the valuable time and energy that was wasted by procrastinating. No experience makes us feel worse than having deliberately undermined our own self-confidence. And, after all the procrastination, our self-judgment about the result of our effort is exactly the same as if we had started immediately.

Preparation without engagement is worthless.
I've noticed that when I've tried to prepare without being engaged in a project, my judgment about this preparation after the project is completed is that it was essentially worthless. The reason is simple: My preparation (without engagement) makes the project more complex than it needs to be. I'm using only a small part of my intelligence and creativity, and I have very little sense of urgency, risk, and excitement. I learn very little, and I gain little or no confidence.

The Advantage: Since procrastination and preparation without engagement are counterproductive and worthless, your advantage lies in immediately engaging with and completing the project—reaching your first 80% as quickly as possible.

Advantage 2

Recognizing that 80% is good enough in 80% of situations, 80% of the time.

Perfectionism puts people into an impossible psychological trap, usually for a lifetime. In a world that is both unpredictable and constantly changing, perfection is virtually an unattainable ideal. Yet, perfectionists are obsessed with achieving "100%" in everything they do. Think of the extraordinary, self-destructive stress this causes inside a person.

Since it's based on an ideal of perfection that has never been, and can never be, experienced, what does "100%" actually mean when we're doing something new? No matter how hard we try, how will we ever know when we've reached 100%? Especially when in Advantage 1, if you accept the thinking, we've already established that our assessment of the result will always be just "80%." The other reason the obsession with 100% is self-destructive is that life only requires an 80% result in 80% of daily situations.

Our "80%" is accepted by others as "100%."
One of the great disabilities that undermines the perfectionistic person is not being able to understand how other people experience and value things. The perfectionist is fixated on achieving 100%, but no one else expects, requires, or will even appreciate this. In 80% of life's situations, an 80% result is good enough to move things forward—and the best 80% result is the one that happens as quickly as possible.

I'll give you an example of this. I'm an experienced layout artist with 30 years of successful work behind me. In my company, Strategic Coach, I initiate most of the printed products we use in The Strategic Coach® Program and those that are sold to the public. Once I've completed the initial layout, a team of graphic designers takes over and completes the projects. Before I created The 80% Approach concept, I used to take whole days, sometimes doing four or five complete drafts, to lay out a single document. The layouts were beautiful—and totally unnecessary. I wanted to do it "100%" before handing it on. But no one except me required this degree of "perfection." The other artists, who were familiar with my style and approach, only needed a rough layout to get clear direction on how to proceed. My obsession with achieving 100% was creating a bottleneck. I've seen countless other examples of this problem in my years of coaching highly successful but stressed-out entrepreneurs. Their insistence on doing everything 100% before passing it on invariably makes them the biggest obstacle to teamwork and productivity in their companies. It increases their stress levels while diminishing the satisfaction they derive from achievement and progress.

When 80% is superior to 100%.

The mental and emotional shift I've undergone makes me certain that in most situations, striving for 80% produces far superior overall results than holding out for 100%. "Most situations" probably means 80% of daily work experiences—where other people's abilities and teamwork play a crucial role. It is in these teamwork situations where "superior overall results" come into play. If I were working in isolation, with no one else necessary to the result, striving for 100% would make sense. But my daily life, with few exceptions, is completely based on teamwork. I find that most other people in today's society would say the same thing.

The Advantage: Because modern life is based on teamwork and utilizes the different abilities of many people, striving for 80% instead of 100% leads to a much faster and superior overall result in 80% of situations.

Advantage 3

Recognizing which 80% of a project each person should handle.

One of the greatest pieces of wisdom I've gained over the past 25 years is that my activities fall into four distinct areas: incompetent, competent, excellent, and what I call Unique Ability®. Incompetent describes those activities that always lead to failure and frustration. Competent activities are those at which I'm able to perform at minimally acceptable standards, but even then it takes enormous effort. Excellent activities are those at which I have superior skills. They come to me easily, but I have no particular passion for them. Finally, Unique Ability is found in those activities where four things are always true: I have a superior skill; I love these activities and can't get enough of them; doing them always energizes me, and other people are energized by my performance; and I keep getting better at these activities. There are no upper limits to my improvement.

Doing only the 80% where I have a Unique Ability.
As I've organized my life increasingly around only those activities where I have a Unique Ability, my success and satisfaction in all areas of life have soared. At the same time, my ability to see where other people have a Unique Ability has dramatically increased. I now see that all the progress in my life lies in linking up my Unique Ability with those of an expanding number of people. But something else is also required for increased success:

It's crucial for me to focus only on my own Unique Ability, and it's equally important for me to focus my Unique Ability on the 80% portion of a teamwork project where my efforts will produce the best and fastest results.

Fast layouts, graphics, copy, and recordings.
The single most important Unique Ability activity I do involves creating new ideas and learning materials for The Strategic Coach Program. I have some very well-developed skills for doing this. One, I design very good layouts that accurately show what the finished materials will look like. Two, I can create graphics that capture the essential ideas of a presentation. Three, I can outline the main copy points or provide finished copy. And, four, I can do audio recordings with little need for rehearsals or second takes. Over the years, I have not only increased my skill level in these activities, but also the speed with which I can complete them. These, then, are the "80% contributions" I make to the production team I work with on a daily basis.

Many other people's Unique Ability and "80% contributions" are required for the finished product.
As important as my skills are, however, they represent just part of the Unique Ability® Teamwork required for the overall result. There is also a project manager, a sound technician, a recording editor, two graphic designers, a final editor-writer, and a print coordinator. All of these other individuals have their own Unique Ability and their own crucial 80% contributions to make. If a project is to be completed in the most productive, successful, and satisfying manner, it's crucial that each of us focuses our Unique Ability on our most important 80% contribution.

The Advantage: Success occurs extraordinarily quickly when all members of a team focus only on their individual Unique Ability, and then focus their Unique Ability on their own "80% contributions" that guarantee the best overall teamwork and results.

Advantage 4

The power of getting the first 80% done as quickly as possible.

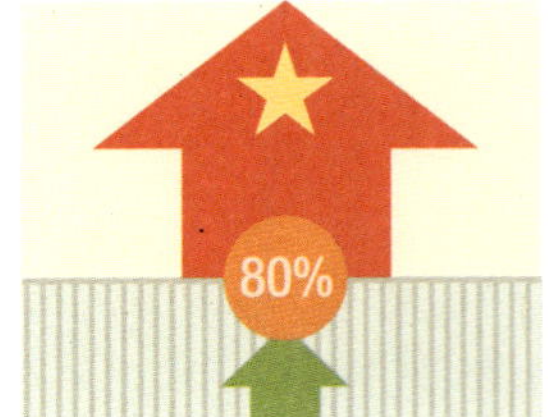

The biggest danger posed by procrastination is that it undermines individual confidence. But there's another danger closely linked to this: Procrastination also prevents teamwork. These two dangers, if not eliminated by The 80% Approach, constantly reinforce each other, making it more and more difficult to increase either individual confidence or teamwork. You can see this in perpetually poor sectors of a society, where a great number of people have long histories of deprivation and failure. An individual growing up in this environment finds it difficult to improve their life. First of all, personal confidence is lacking, but, second, and perhaps most important, teamwork with others is also lacking. Individual improvement in any area of life always depends on teamwork with other self-improving individuals.

In impoverished environments, therefore, individuals procrastinate about taking any action to improve themselves, and they also procrastinate about doing those things that would improve their teamwork with others. So everyone stays poor and depressed.

Successful societies procrastinate the least.
If we turn 180 degrees and examine wealthy parts of any society, we notice an opposite set of forces at work. Because many individuals have long histories of abundance and success, they find it easy to improve their lives. They are constantly increasing their own personal confidence and their teamwork with other self-improving individuals.

Unlike their deprived and depressed counterparts at the opposite end of society, successful people have far less reason to procrastinate because their experience tells them that almost any initiative will produce progress and improvement, both for themselves and for many others.

Why and how the most successful people become more so. Having made this comparison, however, I must state that many highly successful people suffer from procrastination. I say this from having had tens of thousands of hours of in-depth discussions over the past quarter-century with over 6,000 highly successful entrepreneurs. If they still procrastinate, why are they successful? My first response is that they have more confidence, creativity, communication skills, and courage than the general population. But my second response is more important: As successful as they are, they would be ten times more so if they would learn just one simple rule: Always get the first 80% of any project done as quickly as possible.

Immediate increase of confidence and teamwork. Anyone who applies this rule on a daily basis until it's a habit will immediately notice a dramatic change in two areas of experience. One, the elimination of procrastination by doing the first 80% as quickly as possible will provide a burst of personal confidence. This will be increased further by a sense of personal achievement, progress, and improvement. Two, out of this higher personal confidence—and with an actual achievement in hand—it will be easy to attract the teamwork of anyone else who would like to self-improve. In this way, both personal confidence and teamwork increase, leading to greater success for everyone involved. But everything depends on one person taking the lead. By eliminating your own procrastination, you enable others to do the same.

The Advantage: In any situation, you can immediately increase your own personal confidence and teamwork with others by getting the first 80% of any project done as quickly as possible.

Advantage 5

Why focusing on 80% produces bigger and better results than striving for 100%.

The 80% Approach has many different dimensions to it, some of the most important being emotional and psychological. For example, both from my own experiences and from interviewing hundreds of entrepreneurs, I've noticed the following: Striving for 80% seems to produce a better result—that is, a larger and higher-quality result—than striving for 100%.

We've already examined how The 80% Approach generates increased confidence, better teamwork, and faster results. Now, let's look at why it produces a superior result.

Making things worse than they were before.
If someone demands that you achieve 100%—or you demand this of yourself—I can predict what's going to happen to your mind, your body, and your relationships. Mentally, you'll start thinking about failure because that's what anything short of 100% will be. Physically, you'll tense up. You'll become obsessed with 100%, making it difficult to relax or sleep, causing increased strain and fatigue. In addition, you'll become over-demanding with the people working with you, and you'll neglect everyone else who isn't involved with your 100% goal.

Any one of these three problems would undermine the quality of result you're striving for. Combined, they present serious obstacles to creativity, teamwork, productivity, success, and satisfaction. What's worse, not only are you unlikely to achieve 100%, you may fail altogether or produce only a mediocre result. Your striving for 100% may make things worse than before you started. This experience makes it more difficult, instead of easier, to make progress in the future.

Riding the "80% wave" of accelerating confidence.
Striving for 100% increasingly strikes me as working against life, against human nature. It's like sailing against the tide. Striving for an 80% result, on the other hand, seems to let the most powerful forces of human nature work on your behalf. It's like surfing on a big wave. You'll experience constantly growing confidence. Because you're only striving for 80%, you make rapid progress, find it easy, and want to move even faster.

You'll experience increased energy and enthusiasm.
The 80% Approach, as we have discussed, invites and produces much greater teamwork. Everyone involved feels energized by the collective progress and is carried forward by their enthusiasm. You'll experience much higher creativity: Out of their growing confidence and enthusiasm, individuals involved in 80% teamwork maximize their intelligence and Unique Abilities in ways that surpass anything they've achieved before. The image of a whole team being carried forward on a huge, accelerating "80% wave" is very accurate.

80% versus 100%: Community versus isolation.
In the final analysis, the biggest reason why striving for 80% is superior to 100% is what it does to people. The 80% Approach makes them feel like integral, invaluable members of an extraordinary community. The 100% approach makes them feel isolated inside their own fears and uncertainties—unable to utilize other people's abilities and resources.

The Advantage: Because striving for just 80% taps into and utilizes powerful forces of human nature, it always produces a superior result over striving for 100%, which invariably works against human nature.

Advantage 6

The power of delegating the second 80% and beyond—as early and as often as possible.

Since discovering The 80% Approach, here's how I've learned to work on projects. When I analyze how products, such as issues of my quarterly publications, are completed, my own contribution has six parts. In each case, I will give you my pre-80% and post-80% approaches.

My first contribution: the concept.
Before discovering The 80% Approach, I would procrastinate for a long time before committing to a concept. I wanted to make sure that it was absolutely the right one. But at any time, I have four or five concepts in my mind that would work. Operating from The 80% Approach, I now simply choose one and go with it.

My second contribution: the outline.
Prior to The 80% Approach, I would take up to a week to outline a document. This would involve a great deal of detail. At this point, no one else's abilities can be utilized. Now, I can complete a rough outline—all that's really needed—in about an hour. Then I immediately move on to the layout stage.

My third contribution: the layout.
I used to take 15 to 20 hours doing a full-size, page-by-page layout. Sometimes, I would do three or four drafts, which took three workdays. Meanwhile, the whole production team would be waiting—with nothing to work on. And yet, the graphic artists knew what my style

and formats were. They didn't need an extensive layout. So now, after adopting The 80% Approach, I sketch out the entire layout on a single sheet of paper and submit it. This takes, at most, two hours.

My fourth contribution: the text.
Previous to The 80% Approach, I would take whole weeks to complete the text, sometimes doing as many as five drafts. Now, I do a first draft and submit it as quickly as possible. I have skilled editors who can make all the necessary corrections and refinements. This means I can complete an issue in 12 hours. What's interesting is that my fast, single-draft approach is generating a better result—with a two-week savings in overall production time.

My fifth contribution: the illustrations.
Before The 80% Approach, it would have taken me 20 to 30 hours to create the illustrations for the issue. Now, I make rough sketches and submit them to our team of skilled graphic artists within two days.

My sixth contribution: the recording.
Most of my written documents also have an audio component. Before utilizing The 80% Approach, it could take as many as four working days for me to prepare and record a 60-minute presentation. Now, I simply use the printed first draft of the text as my preparation. I go into the studio and record a two-hour presentation in three hours. If my studio team says that it's a good recording, then it is. I seldom do a second recording. By adopting The 80% Approach for each of my contributions to the overall team effort, I've dramatically decreased the time it takes to delegate the next stage to any one of ten other people who have dozens of their own contributions to make. Since I get mine done as quickly as possible, so do they.

The Advantage: Every contribution that you make to a team effort, do it as quickly as possible, so the next steps can be delegated to others as quickly and effectively as possible.

Advantage 7

How eliminating procrastination saves time, improves talent, and transforms emotions.

In the example described in Advantage 6, you can see that I've changed only one thing in each of the six contributions. I've eliminated virtually all procrastination on my part from the overall team process. In doing so, I now complete all my work on the project in a total of about four working days. If I add back in all the procrastination I used to do, the total time my contribution would take could be as much as five to six weeks. But as I have come to realize since adopting The 80% Approach, my own savings are just one small benefit.

Enormous savings of other people's time, energy, and enthusiasm.
When one person eliminates procrastination, getting things done as quickly as possible or even ahead of schedule, it has a dramatic impact on all the other members of the team. A sense of positive urgency is communicated to everyone: *If he or she got it done that quickly, I should do the same thing*. Conversely, procrastination by even one team member sends a message for everyone else to slow down. When I submit my first layout ahead of schedule, it creates the opportunity for the whole team to save time in making their contributions as well. Widespread procrastination in a team makes each individual feel isolated. But when The 80% Approach is widely adopted, everyone feels unified. The energy and enthusiasm of every team member is raised.

Improving each individual's skills.
When a team operating by The 80% Approach achieves a high-

quality result, it also significantly increases the skills of each person on the team. An ineffective, procrastinating team slows down, and actually undermines, the improvement of individual team members. An energized, productive team, on the other hand, dramatically supports and encourages their growth. Perfectionism and procrastination, therefore, are two of the biggest obstacles to the growth and development of all individuals. A team environment in which people use The 80% Approach is devoid of these two obstacles. Each person is liberated to improve at the fastest possible rate.

Counteracting apathy and depression.
The 20th century was marked by a tidal wave of psychological studies, starting with those by Sigmund Freud, that focused on the factors causing individual apathy and depression. Numerous theories have been put forward to explain these conditions, along with prescriptions for curing them—but the one causal factor that is seldom, if ever, mentioned is procrastination. What if the widespread adoption of The 80% Approach were to lead to an equally widespread elimination of apathy and depression in both individuals and groups? I'm totally confident from my own experiences that it would.

I believe that the chronic negative emotions that so many people experience in modern daily life stem from two causes: one, from having a habitual perfectionistic expectation of themselves in daily situations; and, two, from having a deeply ingrained habit of procrastination in dealing with these situations. Each of us can improve the emotional and psychological well-being of society simply by adopting The 80% Approach as our daily operating method. As soon as we do this, it will help others overcome their own perfectionism and procrastination.

The Advantage: By eliminating procrastination, especially in teamwork, we help others save time, improve their talents, and transform negative emotions.

Advantage 8

Why "80% thinkers and achievers" always enjoyably and profitably outperform perfectionists.

If perfectionism actually led to success and higher performance, it might be a useful ideal to pursue. But from my own life, I see very little evidence of this. From 1967 to 1971, I attended St. John's College in Annapolis, Maryland, which is famous in academic circles as "the Great Books school." For four years, I read and discussed many of the classic books of Western civilization, starting with the ancient Greek poet Homer and ending with Einstein's theory of relativity. I went to St. John's simply because I wanted to read all of these books, and I knew I didn't have the discipline to do it on my own. Looking back since I graduated, I've found this education invaluable in helping me to be a better reader, thinker, and speaker, and I'm grateful for the opportunity that St. John's provided.

The mental disease of perfectionism.
For me, the actual education at St. John's was a totally positive experience. But even while I was there, I noticed that this was not true for many other students, many of whom, at that time, were smarter and more articulate than I was. Instead of finding the ideas stimulating, these students found them intimidating.

Worsening paralysis.
As the years at St. John's went by, I noticed many students becoming more apathetic, depressed, and fearful of going out into the world. In visits back for reunions, I've discovered the reason. Whereas I used the books as calisthenics to stretch and develop my mind, many of them used them as timeless, sacred ideals to worsen the condition of

chronic perfectionism they already suffered from even before they had entered college.

The lesson: become a great thinker myself.

The single most important lesson I gained from reading the great thinkers was that I was supposed to become a great thinker myself. The single most important lesson the perfectionistic students learned was that it was impossible for them to ever do anything significant with their lives. Nothing they would ever think, say, or do would have any importance compared with the achievements of the great poets, historians, theologians, prophets, heroes, philosophers, mathematicians, scientists, playwrights, and novelists whom they had studied and discussed. For many of them, the focus of their lives became to worship the books and their authors, not to become significant, influential thinkers and leaders themselves. I find it ironic that they had the benefit of an extraordinary four-year educational opportunity and used it to further paralyze themselves from being creative achievers for their lifetimes.

The great thinkers and doers were "80% people."

There is a further irony. My sense is that my former classmates are convinced that the "god-like" authors of the great books were perfectionists, striving to achieve 100% in every aspect of their lives. After much reading and thinking about these books, I've come to the opposite conclusion. I think the great impact of these thinkers came from the fact that most of them were striving for 80%. They did this for whole lifetimes, and that's why their achievement was so great. If I use a military analogy, perfectionists may win a few battles every now and then, but "80% thinkers and achievers" always win all of the wars. Not only do they overwhelmingly outperform perfectionists, they derive ever greater and growing enjoyment and satisfaction from their efforts.

The Advantage: By adopting The 80% Approach in all daily situations, over a lifetime, you will enjoyably and profitably outperform all the perfectionists you encounter in private and public life.

The Self-Managing Future

The benefits of ever-expanding 80% teamwork within an organization that is increasingly free of perfectionism and procrastination.

In this very small book, I believe I've captured a very big idea for the 21st century. The global population has now crossed seven billion, so there are a lot of possibilities for unique creativity and cooperation around the world in the years and decades to come. The 80% Approach can provide an extraordinary achievement capability to motivated and entrepreneurially-minded men, women, and children in every kind of situation and circumstance. And this achievement can start happening right away.

The systematic focus on the 80% advantages and their increasing use on a daily basis leads to a remarkable increase of self-management on the part of individuals, teams, and organizations.

If you are already a self-managing individual, The 80% Approach will immediately provide you with an increasing ability to respond creatively to unpredictable challenges and opportunities in all areas of your personal and work life.

Going further, your use of The 80% Approach, and sharing it with others, will enable you very quickly to create an entire work team of self-managing individuals. It is conceivable that in the near future, everyone you interact with will also approach all of their work with the 80% attitude. As a result, the whole team will take a jump in terms of progress, performance, and results. What's more, everyone involved in this self-managing team will love the experience of working and growing together. All of the work will be increasingly satisfying and significant for everyone who engages and contributes to the team.

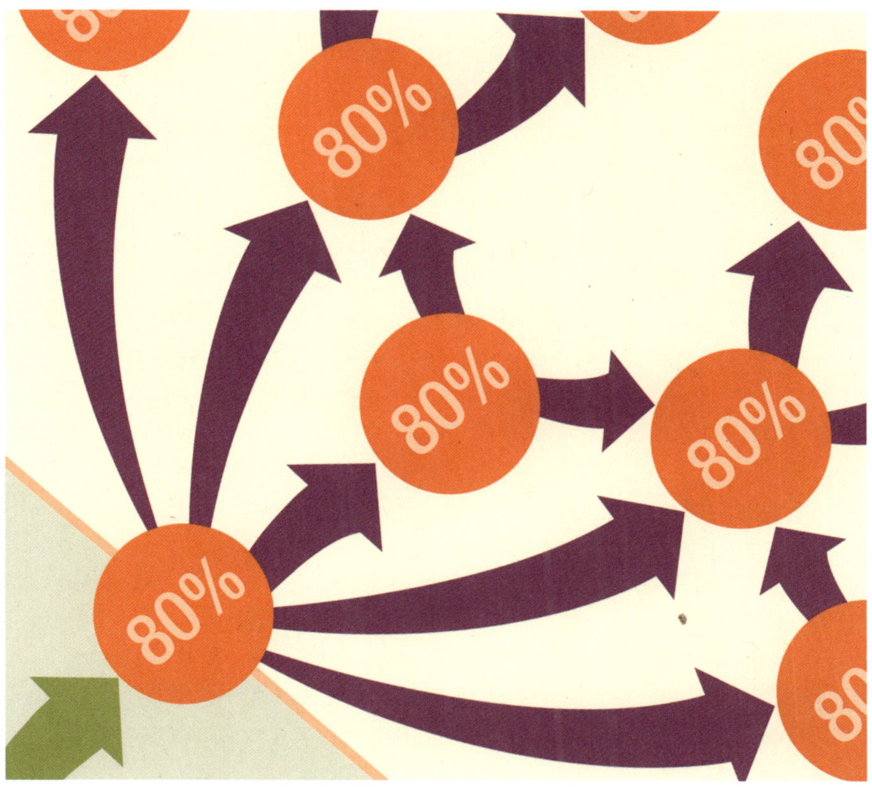

Let's think even further than a single individual, beyond a single team, to a whole organization.

Imagine a growing organization that is made up of an increasing number of self-managing teams. It's easy to see—with everyone freed up from the paralysis of self-defeating perfectionism and procrastination—that each individual's experience within such a self-managing organization would be characterized by high morale, powerful momentum, increasing motivation, and a multiplication of success and importance in whatever industry or profession they're in.

Countless, rapid improvements.
What I've just described very briefly at the individual, team, and organizational levels is how The 80% Approach develops and expands in the world. The most important development here is the self-managing organizations, making countless and rapid 80% improvements, all of them taking advantage of the exponential new capabilities, resources, and opportunities that are being created by information technology.

Before moving forward, however, let's just pause for a moment to consider why some individuals and organizations might not choose, or be able, to take advantage of The 80% Approach in today's world.

The single negative reason here is bureaucratic thinking.

Throughout most of the 20th century, the appropriate development path for individuals within industrial-based societies and economies involved bureaucratic attitudes and work methods. The growing popularity and proliferation of The 80% Approach, therefore, will call into question the practices of many traditional management structures that can all be lumped under the general category of "bureaucracy"—where perfectionism and procrastination are completely entrenched. In order to take advantage of The 80% Approach, individuals will need to leave these bureaucratic organizations in order to be increasingly surrounded by people who are open to the attitudes described in this book.

In this century, dominated by the proliferation of information technology in the crucial activities of every industry, profession, and sector, the appropriate attitudes and capabilities are all entrepreneurial rather than bureaucratic, and The 80% Approach is the best path to individual progress and success.

Tips for getting started right now.
If you are just starting to take advantage of this new 80% way of

thinking, communicating, and taking action, here are eight things you can start doing today and tomorrow:

- **Always be clear and confident about why any new project or initiative is important to you before taking action.** Unless it's exciting and motivating to you, don't get involved. If you find yourself in a situation where you are compelled to get involved in activities you don't enjoy, with people you don't like, make your most important project getting out of this situation as quickly as possible.

- **Focus on just getting three important 80% actions done on any given day, and consider anything more than this a bonus.** Never make a long list of things to do, either in your personal or work life. Simply identify the three most important things to achieve at the beginning of each day, hold yourself accountable for reasonable progress, and achieve it. Then celebrate your movement forward and repeat the same process tomorrow.

- **Do everything well enough, but as quickly as possible, so that someone else can quickly take your projects and initiatives further.** The biggest purpose of The 80% Approach is to surround yourself with teamwork as quickly as possible. You are very good at certain things, but in order to achieve significant progress and results, you need other people who possess the abilities you lack. As quickly as possible, get these other abilities engaged on your behalf.

- **Never have a meeting with others until someone in the group has already completed a first 80% initiative that others can contribute to.** Remember, "meetings" are the main bureaucratic strategy for suppressing individual initiative and for preventing and slowing down organizational progress and change. In The 80% Approach world, a meeting should never happen unless one individual has already started making progress in the area to be discussed.

- **If it's your project, think things through on your own, make**

maximum possible decisions, and start taking immediate actions before any kind of meeting. Don't waste other people's time unless you have some committed progress and achievement to show them. Never ask other people to supply you with motivation and commitment that you don't already have yourself.

- **If you are stuck on any project, ask yourself why you're still doing it.** If you don't have an answer, take the project off your list. Right now, you may be able to cross off and quickly eliminate many projects where you feel a sense of negative obligation rather than positive commitment.

- **If you're stuck on a project and are still committed to it, identify the fastest and easiest action that will get it moving again.** Then do it. Here's a prediction: Every situation in your life where you feel stuck is the result of your wanting to achieve a 100% result. In other words, you're demanding perfection, and that's why you're procrastinating. Whatever it is, scale it back to a first 80% achievement and result that you can start right away and get finished in a very short period of time. That's how to get "unstuck" in any area of your life and work.

- **On a continual daily basis, surround yourself with more and more people who enjoy and are good at operating according to The 80% Approach.** There are seven billion people on the planet, but you don't need them all. In fact, you may need only a few, or a dozen, to make incredible individual and organizational progress in the months and years ahead. But they have to be the right kind of individuals with the right attitudes and abilities. They have to be "80% people."

The systematic daily empowerment of individuals, teams, and organizations, with corresponding liberation from the paralysis of perfectionism and procrastination, is possible with the eight advantages of The 80% Approach.

The 80% Approach only requires a revolution of one person deciding to use it in daily life. Then the revolution will spread to others.

I'm talking about you as the revolution. Your use of The 80% Approach will begin making things more creative and productive within a short period of time. Personal clarity, confidence, and capability will immediately increase in both your personal and work life. Just as a personal example, I wrote this book using The 80% Approach. Instead of writing a thesis of several hundred pages, I just produced something very short. Instead of laboring alone on this book for months and years, it took me less than a week to write and design it, and my team published it in two weeks, with others' help outside of our organization. Everybody on my team and throughout my company is committed to the daily use of The 80% Approach. Immediately upon finishing this book, you can begin making significant progress by applying The 80% Approach to everything you're doing right now, and in all of your teamwork with other people, regardless of your situation. Everyone responds positively to people who get things started and done quickly, who put them in the best possible situation to take their own actions and make their own progress.

Everyone on the planet deals with the obstacles and paralysis caused by perfectionism and procrastination. The vast majority of us would like to find ways of bypassing all of the negativity caused by these mental traps. Thousands of entrepreneurially-minded leaders and their support teams have already increased their productivity and profitability by 10x simply by adopting The 80% Approach in all of their daily creativity and cooperation. I invite you to join this growing community.

Where growth-minded entrepreneurs build their Self-Managing Companies.

After personally coaching more than 6,000 business owners since 1974, I have discovered two fundamental truths about growth-minded entrepreneurs:

One, they are fundamentally motivated throughout their lives by the possibility of greater freedom in four areas: Time, Money, Relationship, and Purpose. Entrepreneurism for them is about transforming their entire lifetime, and their company is the unique structure and process they continually develop and expand in ways that multiply their four fundamental freedoms.

Two, these successful entrepreneurs all want to have a unique, custom-designed structure and process that increasingly becomes a Self-Managing Company. In other words, they want an organization that enables them to focus on what they love doing most, directed by a vision of an always bigger and better future, and managed by a growing team of project and process managers who continually make the overall enterprise more productive and profitable.

In today's world, Strategic Coach is the number-one place where entrepreneurs from 60 different industries continually develop and expand their Self-Managing Companies.

The vast majority of entrepreneurs in the 21st century are striving for greater freedom but find themselves increasingly trapped and paralyzed in haphazard business systems that make their futures more uncertain while making their overall lifestyles more unsatisfying.

This lack of freedom and a future is unfortunate because these individuals, protected and propelled forward for the rest of their lives within their own Self-Managing Companies, and reinforced by thousands of other like-minded "multipliers" in the Strategic Coach community, could be achieving much greater levels of success, satisfaction, and significance in every area of their business and personal lives.

The 80% Approach is a powerful tool within Strategic Coach, but it is just one of hundreds that entrepreneurs and their teams systematically master to create faster and easier progress. Every one of the Strategic Coach concepts has been tested over the past 40 years through successful daily application by more than 16,000 entrepreneurs who are continually expanding their personal freedoms and their organizational capabilities.

Acceleration and excitement.

As The 80% Approach becomes the daily operating philosophy and methodology within an entrepreneurial organization, the process of becoming a Self-Managing Company® immediately speeds up and is extremely exciting and motivating for everyone involved.

The time is right for you to custom-design and build a unique success structure and process for yourself. The process and structure is The Self-Managing Company. The 80% Approach can be a powerful tool within this operating system. And this 80% tool and hundreds more are exclusively available to successful, talented, and ambitious entrepreneurs within The Strategic Coach Program.

If you would like more information about Strategic Coach, its programs for entrepreneurs, or its many products for entrepreneurial thinkers, please call 416.531.7399 or 1.800.387.3206 in North America or 0800 051 6413 from the UK. Or visit us online at *www.strategiccoach.com*.

Listen to the audio presentation of *The 80% Approach* at *strategiccoach.com/go/80approach*